Grief's Alphabet

Also by the Author

The Tethers (Seren, 2009)

Divining for Starters (Shearsman Books, 2011)

Imagined Sons (Seren, 2014)

The Weather in Normal (Seren, 2018)

As editor

Infinite Difference: Other Poetries by UK Women Poets
(Shearsman Books, 2010)

Linda Lamus, *A Crater the Size of Calcutta*
(Mulfran Press, 2015)

Grief's Alphabet

Carrie Etter

Seren is the book imprint of
Poetry Wales Press Ltd.
Suite 6, 4 Derwen Road, Bridgend,
Wales, CF31 1LH

www.serenbooks.com
Follow us on social media @SerenBooks

ISBN: 978-1-78172-750-8
ebook: 978-1-78172-757-7

A CIP record for this title is available from the British Library.

The publisher acknowledges the financial assistance of the Books Council of Wales.

Cover photograph: Bil Borden courtesy of Getty Images.
Author photograph: Fabrizia Costa.

i.m. Bernadine Etter, 30 July 1945-29 July 2011

Contents

III. Orphan Age

Grief is a cruel kind of education. You learn how ungentle mourning can be, how full of anger. You learn how glib condolences can feel. You learn how much grief is about language, the failure of language and the grasping for language.

Chimamanda Ngozi Adichie, *Notes on Grief*

...and the little blur

the little flicker the little bloom of it on the page *you* which is only to
say he was right the scholar of poetry who insisted that the work

of poetry is the work of preserving the fact of the beloved the *you* of
the beloved the work of poetry is preserving the face of the beloved.

Rick Barot, 'The Boy with a Flower Behind His Ear'

I. Origin Story

Birthday as Adoption Day

I tore open the chrysalis or burrowed out of earth to blink in the shock of light. I took worm from beak and cried alive. I pulsed through river, my gills atremble. I struck shell to sunder. A nurse settled me in your arms, and I—With we I began.

An Adoption in 360°

April 1969

From the back, the couple appear conspirators
huddled together in flight, perhaps robbers
were their clothes not so conspicuous,
the young, balding man in his second-best suit,
the dark-haired woman in a yellow tweed jacket and skirt,
dressed more for church than hospital.

From the front, she carries a swaddled infant,
and both the man and woman's bodies curve to shield it,
though it is April in Illinois and the day mild.

From either side, the three are one.

Bigamy

or her beginning

rural Kentucky, 1945   a fishing shack   as one-room house   one narrow bed, one white oak basket   two Bernadines   in the sounds of the river   *dee dee dee* chickadee   mallards, whooping cranes beaver scratch and squeal   in the shack, barely the sound of breath mother and infant   the bed, the basket   since the revelation staggered   sundered   the mother prostrate on the rickety   how long how long   while the baby   baby melding into basket tender skull flattening   small legs gone stiff   how long how long find them, Great Uncle Paul, find them   lift my mother over your head   teach her how to kick

Namesake

i.m. Alice Flanagan

almost apparition the midnight kitchen   theatre of light
in the house's   the prairie's   utter black

from the stairwell the girl watches   father and great-grandmother
on the yellow linoleum   talk?   circle?   dance?

he merely five-foot-four   yet next to her   at eighty she has
her matchstick bones and   ever-black hair

she leans   no falls   and he catches
he lifts the small of her   into the glow

the ceiling light the night's sun
he bears her to   her last

while the girl oh I return   to bed sleep dream
knowing   not knowing   loss

The Lauras

Cross-legged on the gymnasium floor, I blazed
when summoned by my sister's name, I shone.

Which did I covet more, the lyrical *Laura*
or her blood and with it

the unspoken moniker, *real daughter*?
At nine I'd heard but couldn't explain

bastard. For an afternoon, it was enough
to be mistaken and so newly seen

as the PE teacher muttered, *You Etter girls–*
I can't tell you apart.

First Poem

Lake Shafer, Indiana

Not my first body of water, but my first alone: O of the open mouth.

Back at the campsite, all I called family. Delicious distance.

On the bank I wrote the lake in quatrains, leaned into their pull.

Word by word elixir—

Modie! I called as I resumed as I ran.

Guileless I offered up my journal: *Here is the lake.*

American Dream

Here she comes, fourteen, ripped black t-shirt and purple jeans.

Her father wears a clip-on tie with the company logo.

Eldest of five, she can wield her voice like a bullhorn.

Though so many were laid off, he'd supposed he might be spared.

(*O we were not spared.*)

She bristles. She snicks. Again today bullied, she so hormone.

He drops onto the stair, to one side so she may pass and he may.

She stares at him, grimaces, does not yet know.

He holds his head in his hands. He counts up his dependants.

This is the day that. The weather was spring, rain and what warmth.

The House of Two Weathers, or The Years after the Layoff

The mailman brought a Florida postcard
or a thin white envelope the weight of an anvil.

The potted African violet in the kitchen window
raised its richest purple or drooped.

The mother bustled over the stove
or at the sink stood, staring out.

The tabby lazed on the couch
or crouched under a bed.

Almost cloudless blue or
hailstones the size of golf balls.

Cursing, he pored over the bills,
or he cycled into the prairie.

In laughter or in silence the girls
husked cobs of corn over the bin.

The lasagna tasted of love,
or it tasted of ash.

The moon the moon the moon.

Overdose

Leaning into the bathroom mirror, the teenager wonders at her ears, grown so large and surprisingly spotted, their pink polka'd with white. And when gingerly she strokes a lobe, what velvet!

Ten feet away, nestled into one end of the glimmering blue sofa, her mother.

In the mirror, a darkness abruptly visible, shadow in the shape of a man, an assassin, it can only be.... Whimpering, the girl slumps to the floor, out of his eyeline, and clutches her legs to her chest.

Ten feet away, listening, leaning, half-awake, half-asleep in the living dream, her mother.

Where oh where is the dawn?

Pregnant Teenager and Her Mama

You eat and eat and tremble.
You tremble and eat, and your mother
watches you like a mouse a cat.

She swoops in like a bat.
You hope to be claimed:
she alights beside you.

Your hands turn palms up, apology.
Kangaroo, she plucks and drops you
into the warmth of her pouch.

What'll I do? you think,
no need for speech.
Her tongue's on your fur,

or her love's your skin.
The year's a crucible,
and here she is,

a doe who leads
her fawn to water and waits.
O, how she waits.

Chez Bernadine

after Frank O'Hara's 'Chez Jane'

Have you ever seen such a collection of toy lighthouses? Wood, ceramic, plastic, papier-mâché; the artistic amid the kitsch. They pepper the oak shelves either side of the television, on the likely chance its view of a newly refurbished house or an actor's perfect teeth proves less than satisfying and your best chance of transport lies in the choice of one of these little lighthouses and an imaginative journey it is your turn to supply. Consider that tall white one with the single broad red stripe: standing at its base, facing a sea crashing again and again on the rocks below, feeling the spray misting your face, you. You!

Graduation

the gowns, the flat caps a black lake of graduands / in the stands, parents grandparents siblings lovers / one's foremost in the contrast of colour / ceremony and arrival / and my own parents who somehow / as the presenter neared my name in the list of honors / I scanned to find to see their elated / how did they afford / so when we lined up for photos with the university mascot / those plane tickets their only ever flight / six-foot tall, ten-foot-long bronze bruin / I did not sidle cheek to cheek like those before me / or embrace / I put my neck in the bear's jaws / to make a true picture / how I / how we got here

Cantaloupe

Cantaloupe is the scent of my mother or of those summer mornings
we ate breakfast together, talking lightly of the day ahead,

naming errands, generating links among our
hours and movements, so that by the time we'd finished

eating the wet orange fruit, we knew we parted to thrive and
would rejoin to thrive, day burgeoning into the ease of us

all the days I was back in my childhood home, *home home*
as I called it when I'd returned to my city life,

where at the supermarket I'd heft a cantaloupe to smell
but could not bear to buy, eat it on my own.

The News

In an eighteenth-century English bakehouse,
February rattles the panes,
and on the only radiator I warm a mug
so hot tea won't break it.

Something cries in the cold–
perhaps an infant in the cafe below,
but no, closer–
my own phone.

Crackling across the Atlantic,
my mother's voice.
She says, 'Your father,'
and as one, we fall.

Quadriplegic

From a doctor's office to a hospital biopsy to MRSA to paralysis to coma to rehab to home to rehab to home to hospital to home: so in two years Henry travels.

When the wheelchair saleswoman refers to my father as quadriplegic at a volume he on the porch might overhear, I glare her into stone.

Those years, when I visit, I carry my mother in my palm. When I have to return to England, I gingerly hand her to my strongest sister.

Here is a photo of Henry grimacing as he tries to use a walker. It is our last photo of hope.

Here is a photo of Henry with a cast on his leg after the rehab nurse misaligned the hoist. The choice of neon pink, his last attempt at flair or humour or joy.

In the final days, a wife and five daughters circle the beloved on a hospital bed in the house's front room, this awry, this anything-but-redemption, this ache on an altar to harrowing resignation.

I never say the word.

The Last

When the call came, my mother's hoarse whisper, I raced
as a cheetah races;

I entered a steel bird and became bird,
migrating home

by car, by plane, by coach over four thousand miles
and eighteen hours

until in pitch darkness I reached the house,
the threshold.

There I hesitated, not sitting but standing, teetering
on the thinnest of fences,

afraid not of my ebbing father but beginning
the end, the last

room the last hours the last song the last
of us, us,

father and daughter: and from the fence
I leapt for him.

Heroin Song

When she heard the hospice nurse had poured the last of the morphine into a bag of sand, she wept. Mid-March yet the temperature neared seventy. I rubbed my eyes with fists. Mom wanted her to leave, wanted to sleep. The phone rang every ten minutes. When his breathing changed, I was awakened. I didn't think to hurry. The cats circled and perched, circled and perched. So warm for March, ideal cycling weather. His last breath was a tremendous gasp. I made calls. It was dark. I rubbed my eyes with fists. I didn't think to hurry. The cats watched from the sofa, scattered when the morticians arrived. When his breathing changed, I was awakened. It was two-forty a.m., all dark. She came by at seven or eight. Mom wanted her to leave, wanted to sleep. The temperature nearly reached seventy, his ideal cycling weather. When the men went for the gurney, I kissed him good-bye. He was neither warm nor cold. I rubbed my eyes with fists. I called the hospice nurse, then, hours later, my sisters. Mid-March, Friday the thirteenth in fact. His last breath was a tremendous gasp. My blonde sister arrived first. The phone rang every ten minutes. One cat had gone missing. She came by at seven or eight. I didn't think to hurry. When she heard the hospice nurse had poured the last of the morphine into a bag of sand, then my sister wept.

Widow

The plateau she stands on
extends flat in all directions,
prairie without a crop.

When she looks, he is too
plainly not there.
The sky, whatever the weather,

renders absence vast,
apparently limitless.
This is a fallow field—

who knows what it can bear?

Homing

Back from California, back from England, I with my mother became we. If snow blanketed the yard, we saw a cardinal settle on it briefly, brilliant red sharpening the white. If rain fell, we lingered, enchanted, in the rooms where it could best be heard. In summer, we breakfasted on salted melon, ate corn on the cob with dinner. In winter, orange cinnamon tea fragranced the air. For most lunches we travelled to find another enclave, ideally a booth, where we could relish General Tso's chicken or toasted bagels with red onion cream cheese or BLTs on sourdough, we drank large glasses of iced tea, we talked about how this grandchild/nephew aced the state math test, how this daughter/sister liked her new job as a teaching assistant, and we talked like this for days. I was like that red cardinal on the white lawn, easy in brightness, except I was two: we.

The Last Photograph

a golden shovel on the opening line of Gwendolyn Brooks' 'To Prisoners'

Together we watched TV, or you gazed idly while I
eyed you, widowing. I reached for my phone to call
you back.
                'Smile,' I said, positioning the camera for
the last time. You turned slowly; you
struggled to smile, the lamplight a halo, cultivation
of a minor saint.
                                I took the photo, ignorant of
the effort. Only after your death did I sense the strength
summoned to lift your face, now evident in
the mirror. Blame this photo on the love or the
selfishness of daughters, before they meet the dark.

II. The Brink

Notes for A

Alchemy: how to translate agony into

An ague had her

It advanced quickly, a week between

Arlington Drive, 1974 to 2011, a quarter-acre corner lot overrun with
crabgrass and dandelions come summer

Allotment as in an assumption about justice—i.e. since Dad died early—

Arthritis in her knees and fingers, the ache of winter

A as in the teacher's apple, her aspiration

Always, I thought. Always.

No, Not Norovirus

The doctors said *wait*, said *run its course*, said *give it time*

Where was I?

The doctors put a date on the horizon, a date of relief

The errant daughter an ocean away

The date past, on to the hospital

The phone line fizzed, failed to carry

A colonoscopy the investigation's first step

Hastily I ordered flowers, sent them in my stead

But before the procedure began…

Did she see them before she went in?

Her body become all wound, no breath

Tell me she saw my name

The Body in Pain

The arthritis, the cataract, the gallstones,
a broken wrist, high blood pressure, gum disease—

the body suffers and persists, the body in pain
her only home, so did a doctor even ask

after her organs? Albeit kidneys, eyes, heart
all past use, some reformed alcoholic

might yet have enjoyed her immaculate liver—
drinks rarer than Sundays—she

has life in her yet, I should've claimed, begging
over her spent body for more—

The Last Kiss

In a borrowed coffin, she.

I sat I tipped I slouched on a cold, cold metal chair.

I spoke by weeping and wept by keening.

Her skin touched up artificial orange.

I swayed I lurched I craned.

All my names for her I sang I tried though I saw.

I begged by whisper by knee by tear.

The orange of nasturtium or marigold but not.

After how long I rose and lingered and a last kiss.

Last? Even now there I am.

Arrival

I walk into the house, and everything seems to shimmer. Where is she? What is this house if she is not?

I walk into the house, and I am in the room where we last sat together, her cats Mario and Luigi lounging with us before the TV.

I walk into the house and think I can smell her lasagna: tomato sauce, basil, ground beef, sheets of pasta, mozzarella, cottage, parmesan cheese. I'm so hungry.

I walk into the house and find two of my four sisters and their husbands searching for her will and her solitaire engagement ring.

I walk into the house, the house we moved into when I was five, the house I've traversed in dreams for decades. Even the looseness of the front doorknob, its give as though it has never been installed as tightly as it should have been, feels keenly familiar.

I walk into the house and am ready to call one of her many names.

I walk into the house, and two sisters sit at the dining room table. The business of death.

I walk into the house, and I want to check the cupboards, the fridge, the freezer for the foods she bought for my visits–Spaghettios, Triscuits, Diet Coke–though it is still three weeks before my scheduled stay.

I walk into the house and nearly.

I walk into the house and take off my shoes to feel under my feet the new carpet she wrote about, part of the refurbishment before the sale, before her next, last home with a guest room for me or a grandchild or sister.

I walk into the house, and my sister Nancy says, 'Thank God you're here.'

I walk into the house and wish I could buy it, make it my own.

I walk into the house and remember how she used to keep brown sugar in the fridge, how I'd ferret out a large nugget to dissolve on my tongue.

I walk into the house and see her lighthouses. If I pick one up, will I be transported to its base, she by my side, as we look out on the sea?

I walk into the house, and my brother-in-law is calling the pawn shops.

I walk into the house, and everyone at the dining table rises, as though I am the admiral or officiant of grief.

I walk into the house and see the framed photograph of orange buttercups meadowing a snow-tipped mountain I bought for her from JC Penney when I was twelve or thirteen.

I walk into the house and look askance at the living room as though my father's hospital bed was not collected two years ago.

I walk into the house and learn the ring has been discovered at a pawn shop in downtown Bloomington, its receipt bearing the name of my youngest sister.

I walk into the house and wonder what will spill out if I open the living room closet: my childhood roller skates a purple duffle coat Christmas wrapping paper a wedding dress in a dry cleaning bag how many pairs of shoes the paraphernalia of husband and wife five daughters twelve grandchildren in one cresting wave.

I walk into the house and look down to watch my steps as though on a balance beam.

I walk into the house and wonder about the price of heroin: how long a high does one hocked ring buy?

I walk into the house and listen for John Denver's voice.

I walk into the house and imagine she's in the kitchen or the bedroom or the garage, just a few steps and a pivot and hello hello.

I walk into the house and hear my father's last gasp.

I walk into the house and am tasked with finding the will, writing a eulogy, making the visitation and funeral arrangements, writing an obituary, sorting out her accounts, distributing her belongings, and not falling face first into woe.

I walk into the house and know once I leave I'll never see these rooms again.

I walk into the house and wait for her.

Funeral

In the front pew hazel-haired Laura sways as she weeps

Pale skin palimpsest worn thin by the onslaught

I fold, unfold my poor eulogy as I walk to the lectern

Forty years ago, Laura an infant in a white wicker bassinet

Gleeful flurry of limbs as our mother reached

Alone in the crowded nave two orphans

Widow (2)

In the house of the dead, I foraged.
In the closet, among her few dresses,
she had saved several of his button-down shirts,
but they would not tell me their stories.

For weeks I rummaged and sorted
and, going into the garage,
saw her car. In the trunk, two books:
Facing Loneliness; Cooking for One.

The Blood, Oh the Blood

The month after your death,
the month I searched, gathered, sorted,

begged, wept, argued, and slept,
I bled and didn't wonder.

I bled again and did
and asked why

and though you were everywhere–
the curtains' cornflower meadows,

an Irish novel bookmarked *Best Mum*,
the silvertone watch on the dresser

still improbably ticking
without the company of your pulse–

you didn't answer or
you were the answer,

the loss my body
revolted to bear.

Dreaming of the Dead

indeed forlorn as forsaken in the brusque loss
the hoard of unspoken speech the weather of it

the quickening wind and distant bright
solitary solicitude some self-pity

some unfinished desires frayed threads
stroke one by one between thumb and forefinger

such texture under the slow touch
which is to say a vigour in memory an insistence

awry awake up now I go

Why I Didn't Save One of Her Lighthouses for Myself

In May 2022, the Queenscliff Maritime Museum held a competition for a collective noun for lighthouses.

At last I faced her lighthouses, the smallest the size of my thumb.

In dozens on shelves either side of the TV.

Which Christmas did Nancy and I give her lighthouse calendars?

I could not find one to represent the whole.

All those portals for she who.

A relief of lighthouses.

The Body in Mourning

a body, prostrate   above the duvet, its teal floral

the street's whir of tires, clank of a truck and rumble

which is to say, a species of silence   sound become peripheral

the windows closing out, closing in   October or November's crisp

the body still, eyes open   a soundless, resounding *no*

★

after the disbelief, her bones grew soft   the spine pliable

onto, across the floor   not as though they melted but

like rubber, a curl and bouncing unfurl   whip-snap of sob and shriek

after a day of curving roads   through the Devon green

after the riverside restaurant, summer wine   a reflexive, mundane call

a post-procedure check-in   changing her

bones   at the molecular level   soft, as in askew

★

O leaky body   such water   such flood, mucus and

mascara she'd forgotten   her charred cheeks in the mirror

she hesitated to wash   the natural tattoo

and so stared long to memorise   charred

as though she could flick at it   and her face would crumble

★

the daily waking to   mourning

the white ceiling's plateau   so unlike childhood's white ceiling

its peaks and ridges, a topographical map

patterns, images   but here: nothing

nothing and nothing and nothing   to rise to

the body become stone, the breath   reluctant

*

and after years?   the body's subtler flux

amid the elements: an hour aflame   or drenched

weighty as mineral   deep in earth   or almost

transparent, nearly air   thin linen pinned to string

adrift or aloft   depending on

H Is for Hurtle, J for July

My July hurtles towards Janus:
on the 29th, her death on an operating table
four thousand miles away:
on the 30th, the anniversary of her birth,
but there is no cake, no candles
to burn, no long contemplated amid
hastily purchased presents. I said

hurtle yet could also say hurdle
as I spend the month leaping and
stumbling at the insurmountable.
Look at these skinned knees I might say
to myself. As for hurt,
either I will go into the garden and yank
out the weeds or I will slip
under a duvet and call my cats to join me.

Imagine such a month, the mountaineer's
climb from single to and through double digits.
I loiter in bed, but I, bride to wakefulness, I,
mind rummaging toward world, I,
horizontal lumbering toward
vertical, I, athirst, swallowing
to wet my throat, I—

I hurtle through an air
thick as treacle, whether in the shower
soundlessly keening, whether in the market
knocking a watermelon as she
or searching for cobs of corn still in
the husk I would peel as she set
the water boiling, whether whether whether
all July even sitting in a park and watching
men in white play cricket I hurtle through
the blank, ceaseless corridor of grief.

And so much for July—I write in December.
Lifelong I daughter.

F Is for Fuck This

III. Orphan Age

R Is for Ruby

Such dense fog, day after day, week after week,
I lumbered through after her death.

Abruptly, a glimpse of colour,
dark pink.

It drew me to the glass:
a ruby, her birthstone.

I drifted into the shop, reckoned the cost,
and left

still bereft, yet
a memorial on my finger,

a lodestar I could touch.

The Modie Box

I try to remember all there is to remember.
I labelled a box file The Modie Box,
Modie my first name for her.
Inside, letters, cards, photos, postcards, post-its.
My mind is another Modie Box.
Inside, her fondness for French burnt peanuts;
the time she cried when the radio played
Anne Murray singing 'You Needed Me';
ticket stubs for John Denver and Peter,
Paul, and Mary; the upright piano
she never played, never urged us to learn.
I collect and collect: the novel from her bedside,
bookmark never to advance; the framed photo
of Pope John Paul II that disappeared
from our dining room wall; a predilection for TV's
reality talent shows, home refurbishment.
I cannot stop. Is it too late
to become a better daughter?
Yes, it is too late. Still I.

M Is Usually Memory and Occasionally McDonald's

Walking by a McDonald's in England, I, a whiff of not quite nostalgia.

The fryer oil, the yellow logo, the cheap beef, oh and the Happy Meals.

My mother and I, two large Diet Cokes, the drive thru one of our.

There must be a way to talk about capitalism without disdaining everyone.

After the thrift shops, maybe a shoe store, Dollar Tree, and on home.

How we took ease. Our only thought, thirst. Slaked homeward, again.

Wintering

The warmth of the juncture: my cat's furred back against my leg. By minutes the days are beginning to lengthen. Last week, he had two surgeries in two days. The house grew cold and colder. The curtains remained closed against the faint light, the overcast sky. When I opened the door this morning, sunstruck fog, and in the maple, small birds chirping, chirruping delight? discontent? In the winter tree I could see them, restless, pounce from branch to branch, spurred to movement, spurred to voice. The day would be short, and they would have all of it.

Ode to Tuna Casserole

So much salve comes out of
a tin can: Campbell's Cream
of Mushroom, Cream

of Potato Soup, and don't forget
the tuna itself. You'll also need
wide egg noodles, salt, pepper,

and for the crust, greasy, plain,
crushed potato chips.
Call it mildness run rampant,

call it Midwestern,
call it an homage to
my mother: I am, in a bite,

all ease—

W Is for Wedding

As I sweep into the Bath registry office on no one's arm, I survey the room to see so many friends, former students, my fiancé's relatives, and at the front, standing, smiling, Trevor, in a suit with a burgundy tie to match my Biba dress. As I make my way to the centre aisle, I notice a single empty seat. There my mother is and isn't, and I pause, acknowledge her presence and absence as I take a step, then another, toward joy.

Ouroboros

In a white clapboard house, the stillness of a weekday afternoon. Mother and three-year-old daughter on the couch, no space between them. What was the name of the book?

Here, the shrillness of the telephone. A mustard-coloured Bakelite on the kitchen wall. The mother scrambles up, leaves the open book in the girl's hands.

The pleasing weight of the large, illustrated pages. How many times has this book been read? As she speaks the words, does the girl read or recite?

Do you suppose your first memory will be your last?

Do you believe, on the girl's deathbed so many years later, she'll sit next to her mother again on that gold velveteen couch and feel the warmth of her body, her voice as she reads?

Will the phone even ring?

Nightlife

We are at the crazy golf in Bath about to play the windmill hole, though, as it's been sixteen and a half years since I last played crazy golf, the windmill may be as fictitious as the dream it appears in, yet my mother isn't a fiction, only her aliveness is, and indeed I can vouch for the red cotton top she wears, as it's one of the three I kept for myself in that long August of sorting her everything and generally bearing either my sisters' suspicion or disdain for it. Anyway, my passportless American mother, alive at the Bath, England crazy golf and drawing the putter back, pauses to gauge the distance along the passage through the windmill to the hole and its cup of glory. I'm not sure whether my mom studied physics in school, but something in the focus of her gaze makes me think my couch-loving, fleshy mama has, in this new existence, an inner sportswoman, and yes, of course yes, with a graceful swing she lands a hole in one. My mother beams, her ruddy face alight for a long beautiful second before I wake. I don't believe in the hereafter or Heaven, but tonight I'll go to bed at the exact same time, wear the same leopard-print pyjamas, and give the same affectionate good night to my unwitting husband, to ensure my resumption of the most delicious game, in which undoubtedly—undoubtedly—the next hole in one will be mine.

The Long Summer

Come July,
roses, lavender, sweet pea–
tipsy I go
on colour, on perfume,

till brought to a pause
at a pool of silence, memory–
your face
floats up.

Come your birthday,
I wade in.

Instructions for the Glimpse

Stare out the window, past the geranium and dormant orchid, when washing knives.

There: the jolt of injury, a bead of blood, a shudder back into body and its unspoken hungers.

Part memory, part presence, the sharp perception of the one who was. In this kitchen. In this now tenderly suspending time.

Soon you will either drift into memory–her care of cooing, bandage, attention–or into life, turning on the tap to rinse the wound.

Stay. She is so close, so nearly palpable, and you rise into yourself, alone and not alone, with and without. You are a sunflower or a startled doe or a crying child, and she is the air you breathe.

Grief's Alphabet

A is for a teacher's typical Red Delicious, her lifelong, unattained ambition, while
B is she herself, Bernadine, the only one I've known.
C could be Carrie, if she hadn't, on adoption day, named me Carol.
D, daughter, is forever, which entails
Etter, also the name of a Swiss cherry liqueur I long to taste.
F could name the doctors' folly,
giving her diagnosis as norovirus and looking no further until
hospital, just weeks before my expected visit. Yes, it's all about me,
insolent, indolent ingrate of a daughter,
joylessly
keening eleven years
later.

Modie, mommy, mother, maman,
norovirus it wasn't, and your colonoscopy was
over before begun. I was in Devon,
oblivious, again. It was supposed to be a routine
procedure, and yet. And yet, back from dinner, I
quickened, called, just to check in, and in seconds
recoiled,
shuddered, screamed, and wept.

T is tally, my tally of regrets. What can I say to
you in death? Is there any
virtue in
wielding this clumsy dirge on an old Fisher Price
xylophone? Modie, I'm getting old without
you, and yet somehow I'm an exuberant
zaftig at an improbable zenith, only–*only*–because of you.

Ghost

I stand just outside the house, on the north hill of Bath, and look down into the valley. I nod at Solsbury Hill and Bathampton, as though in greeting. The photo captures the moment I raise my arm to point them out, to her standing beside me, to her who never stood here, who never came to England. My mouth is open: there are so many words.

Reincarnation as Seed

begin in air, aloft   float   drift   in an early mist   a few weeks after the season's last frost   so the soil has begun to ease   and yes! a crevice   you fall into   a kind of exhalation   amid and soon secure   as you wait, a timeless, thoughtless   until   rain!   now to absorb   expand swell with water   and now crack! open   into root and shoot   grow, grow toward light   drink it   and O, my dear mother   bask

Happy
Birthday

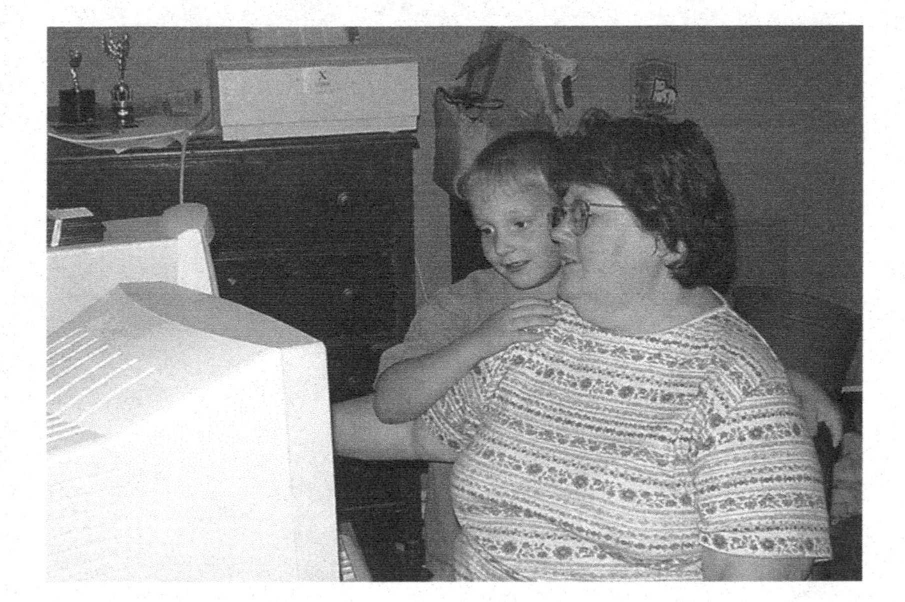

Acknowledgements

My gratitude to the editors of the following publications, in which some of these poems appeared: *berlin lit, Blackbox Manifold, English, The English Review, Lighthouse, The Mackinaw, Molly Bloom, The Moth, New Walk, Plume, Poetry Ireland Review, Poetry Wales, The Rialto, Shenandoah, The Warwick Review, Wildness, women : migration : poetry [an anthology]* (Dwarf Stars, 2016), *Zocalo Public Square.*

My thanks to all the poets who responded to one or more of these poems independently or in the Helyars and South Bank workshops: Moniza Alvi, Fiona Benson, Kate Bingham, Patrick Brandon, Matt Bryden, Julia Copus, Claire Crowther, Jane Draycott, Christina Dunhill, Annie Freud, Martha Kapos, Jenny Lewis, Katy Mack, Daniel Sluman, John Wedgwood-Clarke, Susan Wicks, and Jackie Wills. Thanks to Jinny Fisher for a warm space to write and revise on a painfully cold winter weekend, Matthew Leigh for his advice and encouragement, and to the Prose Poetry Project for a virtual space to share some of these poems. I am also grateful to my editors at Seren, Zoë Brigley and Rhian Edwards, for their support. Thanks too to the friends and students who sustain me with their faith and encouragement–I am so fortunate.

My utmost gratitude to my husband, Trevor Lillistone.

About the Author

Carrie Etter lived for nineteen years in Normal, Illinois, before moving to southern California in 1988. She has lived in England since 2001 and published four collections of poetry: *The Tethers* (Seren, 2009), winner of the London New Poetry Prize; *Divining for Starters* (Shearsman, 2011); *Imagined Sons* (Seren, 2014), shortlisted for the Ted Hughes Award for New Work in Poetry; and *The Weather in Normal* (UK: Seren; US: Station Hill, 2018), a Poetry Book Society Recommendation. She also edited *Infinite Difference: Other Poetries by UK Women Poets* (Shearsman, 2010) and Linda Lamus's posthumous collection, *A Crater the Size of Calcutta* (Mulfran, 2015). She also writes short stories, essays, and reviews. Since 2022, she has been a member of the creative writing faculty at the University of Bristol.